A New True Book

THE TLINGIT

By Alice Osinski

CHILDRENS PRESS ®

CHICAGO

Library of Congress Cataloging-in-Publication Data

Osinski, Alice.
 The Tlingit / by Alice Osinski.
  p.   cm. — (A New true book)
 Includes index.
 Summary: Describes the traditional life-style, arts
and crafts, changing land, and modern life of the Tlingit
Indians.
 ISBN 0-516-01189-8
 1. Tlingit Indians—Juvenile literature. [1. Tlingit
Indians. 2. Indians of North America.] I. Title.
E99.T6085   1990   89-25345
973:.04972—dc20   CIP
                                                           AC

**For Tlingit children who continue to
dream their ancestors' dreams**

PHOTO CREDITS

Photographs Courtesy Alaska State Library—Winter & Pond
Collection—12 (left #PCA 87-237 and right #PCA 87-182), 13
(left #PCA 87-244 and right #PCA 87-35), 14 (#PCA 87-333,c.1),
20 (#PCA 87-64), 21 (#PCA 87-106), 22 (left #PCA 87-176), 23
(left #PCA 87-39,c.1), 31 (#PCA 87-65), 38 (#PCA 87-334), 39
(top left #PCA 87-242 and bottom left #PCA 87-326 and right
#PCA 87-139), 44 (left #PCA 87-200 and right #PCA 87-7)

© Reinhard Brucker—22 (right), 24 (4 photos), 35 (2 photos)

Joan Dunlop—8 (right), 32, 41

Virginia Grimes—6 (bottom)

Reprinted with permission of The New Book of Knowledge, 1989
edition. © Grolier Inc.—5

Historical Pictures Service, Chicago—37

Museum of the American Indian—26 (bottom right #4611), 36
(right #4222)

R/C Photo Agency—© J.M. Halama, 10 (bottom), 16 (2 photos)

Chris Roberts Represents—© Slocomb, 2

Shostal Associates/SuperStock International, Inc.—8 (bottom
left); © Ernest Manewal, 19 (top right), 23 (right)

Bob & Ira Spring—Cover, 6 (top), 7, 10 (top), 15, 17, 19 (left and
bottom right), 26 (left and top right), 27, 29 (2 photos), 33, 36 (left),
40 (2 photos), 42, 43 (2 photos), 45

Tom Stack & Associates—© Leonard Lee Rue III, 8 (top left); © Jeff
Foott, 9

COVER: Chilkat dancers use historic Chilkat blankets in authentic
tribal house.

TABLE OF CONTENTS

COMING TO ALASKA

Along the southeast coast of Alaska a group of American Indians have been fishing for thousands of years. They call themselves the Tlingit (pronounced *klink-it*).

Ancestors of the Tlingit came to Alaska thousands of years ago, when much of the land was covered by large sheets of ice called glaciers. Today, Tlingit

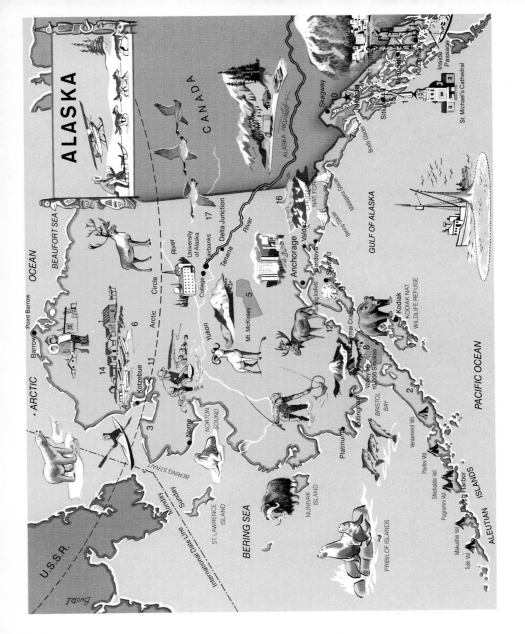

people live in many
communities in Southeast
Alaska. The society is
divided into two groups
called Raven and Eagle.

Alaska has thick cedar forests (below) and beautiful sunsets (above).

A LAND OF PLENTY

Southeastern Alaska is a good place to live. It has a mild climate year-round. There are plenty of animals to hunt, fish to catch, and berries to eat. The nearby forests provide wood for fuel and for building houses.

The village of Hoonah, Alaska

Fish, especially salmon, is a main source of food for the Tlingit. Salmon can be eaten fresh or dried. Often, it is cooked over a smoking fire to give it a special flavor.

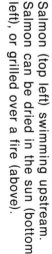

Salmon (top left) swimming upstream. Salmon can be dried in the sun (bottom left), or grilled over a fire (above).

In the past, the Tlingit set up fishing camps in the spring and fall. They speared the salmon as they swam upstream, or caught them in nets or traps. Today, the Tlingit catch salmon with seine nets and gill nets. Sometimes they use fishing

A woman netting fish (left).

9

Small canneries, like the one (above) prepare fish for market. Right, a man bones a halibut.

poles. Many Tlingit sell their catch to big companies.

In addition to salmon, the Tlingit catch halibut, herring, cod, and crabs. Along some rivers, fish called eulachon are gathered in nets. A tasty oil comes from the eulachon. Some people like to dip their food in this oil.

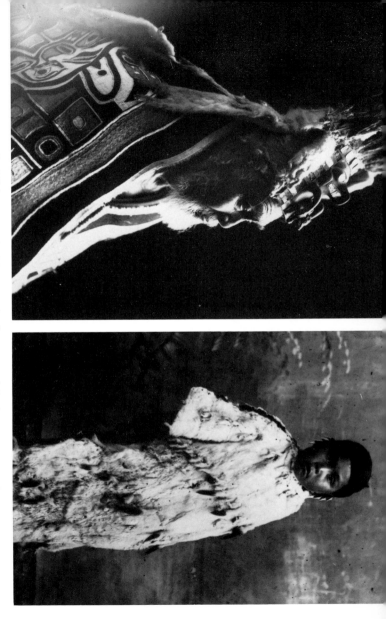

The old man and child wear clothing made from goat hair, animal furs, and bird feathers.

In the past, hunting was very important to the Tlingit. They hunted sea lions and otters along the rocky shores. Those who lived inland hunted mountain goats, bear, and deer. From

Items that Tlingits wear or carry identify them as members of a certain clan. The rattle that the man on the left is carrying shows that he belongs to the Raven clan.

these animals, they fed and clothed their families. Because hunting was such dangerous and necessary work, good hunters were respected.

VILLAGE LIFE

The ancestors of today's
Tlingit people lived very
busy lives. In the summer
and fall of each year, they
set up temporary fishing
camps to gather food. Then,
before winter set in, they

Chief Shakes's tribal home is on a tiny island in the inner harbor of Wrangell.

returned to their villages.
There, several families lived
together in large houses
made of cedar.

The houses were painted
with colorful pictures of
animals and birds. Sometimes,
the Tlingit made carvings

Tlingit homes painted
with colorful designs

of animals on the wooden
posts that supported the
houses, or on the doorways
and entrances. Tall wooden
carvings, called totems,
stood in front of the houses.
Some totem poles were
twenty feet high. They were
carved with brightly painted

Chief Kadashan totem poles on Shakes Island

figures that represented a family, a clan, birds, or animals. Totem poles recorded family and clan history.

After a totem pole was raised, a ceremony was held. Someone would tell the story of the carved figures on the pole and explain why they were placed in a particular order.

In many Tlingit communities

Family and clan histories are recorded on totem poles.

today, you can see beautifully carved cedar houses and totem poles.

BASKET WEAVING AND WOOD CARVING

During the cold, rainy months of winter, Tlingit families wove blankets, mats, and baskets. They also carved beautiful wooden boxes, tools, and masks.

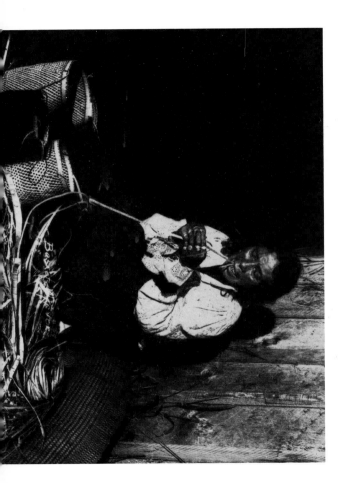

These basket weavers in Sitka, Alaska, were photographed in 1897.

The Tlingit were very skillful at making containers from the fibers of grasses and the roots of plants. First they soaked the fibers in water to soften them. Then the women skillfully wove the fibers into baskets. Some baskets were used to carry

things or for storage.
Others were woven so tightly that
they were waterproof.
These were used for cooking.

Mats woven from strips of
cedar bark had several uses.
Some were used in women's
clothing, or as bedding.

Large mats were hung from the ceiling to separate different living areas.

Women wove blankets from goat wool and cedar bark. The designs were created by the men.

Designs on many blankets and robes represented the bear, the whale, or the raven.

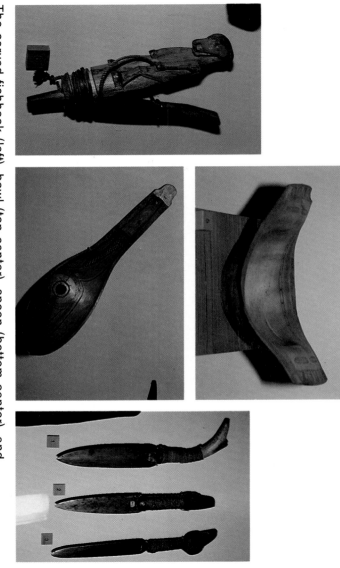

24

Boxes made from cedarwood were used for storing food and household items. They were beautifully carved and painted. The Tlingit also carved and painted their tools, weapons, fishing hooks, and even their dishes.

STORYTELLING

During the winter, the Tlingit also spent time recording the important events of the past year. They did not write down their history. Instead, they used storytelling and plays that included dancing to pass down their history and their values to their children. Most dancers were dressed as creatures of the sea and the forest, especially the raven, the bear, and the killer whale. While a drummer beat his drum, the dancers would imitate the movements of the animals. A certain combination of movements

Dancers wear clothing, masks, and headdresses that represent the animals they imitate, such as the raven (top right) and killer whale (above right). Chief Kat-Lean wore the raven headdress during a fight he had in 1802 with the Russians at Old Fort Sitka.

told a particular story. As they danced, singers or storytellers told the stories. Today, the Tlingit still perform these dances and tell the same stories their ancestors told so long ago.

27

GIFT GIVING

The biggest event of the winter for the Tlingit was a feast called a potlatch. Sometimes it lasted four days or more. Families gave these feasts to mark an important event in their lives such as the birth or death of a family member, or some special achievement. During a potlatch, there was much dancing, storytelling, and gift giving. The gifts included food, blankets, canoes, and

People celebrate the raising of a totem pole.

even fishing rights. The number of gifts showed how generous the families were and how important the event was to them. In most Tlingit communities today, potlatches still take place.

CARVING A CANOE

The Tlingit have always
made their living from the
sea. Those who lived a long
time ago hunted and fished
from small canoes. Large
canoes took them on long
trading trips, to special
feasts, or to war. Often, they
traveled great distances to
trade with other Indians.
Among the items they traded
were fish oil, shells, copper,
furs, carvings, and woven
blankets.

Building a canoe was a
special event in the village.
Although many people
helped to make the canoe, a
master carver was in charge.
He chose the men who went
into the forest to chop down
the red or yellow cedar tree.

Then he watched over all the stages of building the canoe.

After the tree was hollowed out, it was carried to the water's edge. There it was carefully carved and shaped so that it would handle easily and move smoothly through the water.

Design on a Tlingit canoe

Finally, it was given a name and painted with family emblems, or crests.

Today, the Tlingit still build colorfully carved canoes, but most Tlingit families fish in large modern boats that have motors.

RELIGION

Tlingits have always been closely tied to nature. Their beliefs have centered around God as the creator of life and around spirit helpers who have power to influence such things as weather, hunting, and healing the sick.

Shamans wore masks during certain ceremonies.

In traditional Tlingit society, special people, called shamans, would contact spirit helpers for guidance.

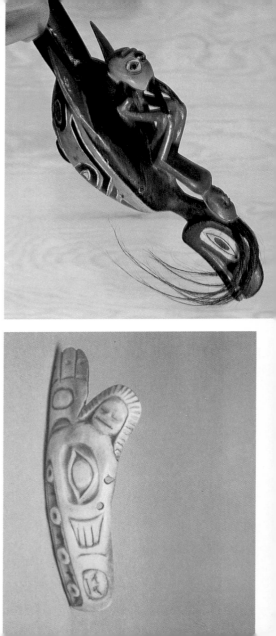

A wooden rattle (left) and a shaman's eagle-head charm carved from ivory (right)

During certain ceremonies, shamans would wear special masks and robes. They would sing songs and request favors from the spirit helpers.

Today, many Tlingit communities are Christian. Yet, traditional beliefs still influence their lives.

Vitus Bering

THE CHANGING LAND

In the 1700s, Vitus Bering, a Danish explorer working for the czar of Russia, came to Alaska. He claimed all the land for Russia. Before long, Russian fur traders began building forts and setting up trading companies. They took the land away from the Tlingit.

The Treadwell gold mine in 1899

The Tlingit fought bravely
to keep their land. Many died
in battle. In 1867, Russia sold
Alaska to the United States.
In the 1870s, gold was discovered
in southeast Alaska. Soon
thousands of people came

to mine the gold and live in Alaska. Missionaries built churches and schools. The United States government began to build schools, too. All these events changed the Tlingit way of life.

These pictures show how Tlingit clothing changed after the Tlingit were ruled by outsiders.

Tlingit elders continue to teach the history and customs of their people.

MODERN LIFE

Today, Tlingit-Americans have a modern life-style but the old ways are mixed with the new. Many Tlingit still live in small villages and towns along the coast. They live by logging, fishing, and hunting. Others own

Sitka, Alaska

businesses in large cities
such as Sitka and Juneau.
Many work as artists,
teachers, lawyers, and
priests, and many work for
the government.

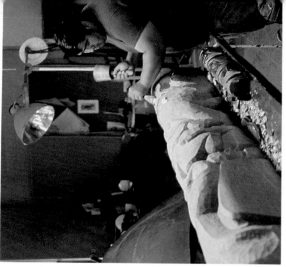

Today, modern Tlingit artists (below) continue to carve the magnificent totem poles that their ancestors carved in prehistoric times (left).

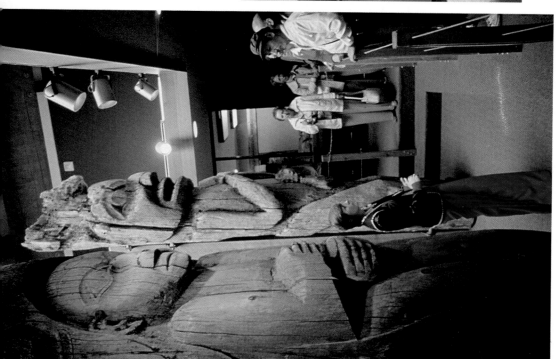

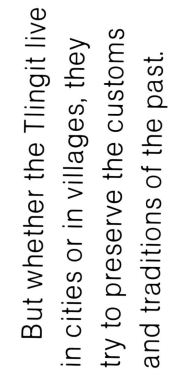

But whether the Tlingit live in cities or in villages, they try to preserve the customs and traditions of the past.

Tlingit dancers in the early 1900s

Long ago, ancestors of the modern Tlingit fought to keep their land and their customs. Today, as Americans, the Tlingit are still struggling to preserve them. They are working together to pass laws to protect the land and their right to use it. They are

sending their children to schools that will prepare them for the future while their elders work to preserve the beauty of their past.

WORDS YOU SHOULD KNOW

Bering, Vitus (BAIR • ing   VHY • tuss) — Danish navigator who first sighted Alaska in 1741

cedar (SEE • der) — a tall tree of the pine family, noted for its fragrant wood

clan (KLAN) — a group of families

climate (KLY • mit) — the average weather of a place over a period of years

crest (KRESST) — an emblem representing a family or other group

emblem (EM • blem) — a picture symbolizing a group or an idea

feast (FEEST) — a meal celebrating a special event

gill nets (GIHL   nehts) — flat nets that hang vertically in the water

glacier (GLAY • sher) — large body of ice covering a land surface

halibut (HAL • ih • but) — a large flatfish

herring (HAIR • ing) — a food fish

Juneau (JOO • no) — a city and port in southeastern Alaska

otter (AH • ter) — a fish-eating mammal

potlatch (PAHT • latch) — a feast marked by the giving of gifts

preserve (pri • ZERV) — to keep

Russia (RUH • sha) — a former empire, now the Soviet Union

seine nets (SAYNE   NEHTS) — large, vertical nets used to enclose the fish when the ends are pulled together

shaman (SHAH • min) — a person who uses special powers

temporary (TEM • puh • rayr • ee) — for a limited time

Tlingit (KLINK • it) — American Indians who live in southeastern Alaska

totem pole (TOH • tem POHL) — a pole carved or painted with symbols that represent a family history

INDEX

About the Author

After teaching American Indian children for seven years in Pine
Ridge, South Dakota, and Gallup, New Mexico, Ms. Osinski
launched her career in writing. She has developed bicultural
curricula for alternative school programs in South Dakota and New
Mexico. Her articles and children's stories have appeared in
textbooks for D.C. Heath and Open Court. She has written several
books for Childrens Press in the True Book series, including The
Sioux, The Chippewa, The Eskimo, The Navajo, and The Nez Perce.